# Looking After Our Environment

By Nicolas Brasch

Pearson Australia
(a division of Pearson Australia Group Pty Ltd)
707 Collins Street, Melbourne, Victoria 3008
PO Box 23360, Melbourne, Victoria 8012
www.pearson.com.au


First published 2014 by Pearson Australia
2018 2017 2016
10 9 8 7 6 5 4 3 2

Publisher: Dian Faulisi
Project Manager: Michelle Thomas
Editor: Margaret Trudgeon
Cover & Series Designers: Jenny Grigg and Anne Donald
Designer: Norma van Rees
Copyright & Pictures Editor: Katy Murenu
Mac Operator: Rob Curulli
Illustrator: Fiona Lee
Printed in Australia by the SOS Print + Media Group

ISBN 978 1 4860 0846 9
Pearson Australia Group Pty Ltd ABN 40 004 245 943

**Acknowledgements**
We would like to thank the following for permission to reproduce copyright material.
The following abbreviations are used in this list: t = top, b = bottom, l = left, r = right, c = centre.

AAP: Jenny Evans, p. 11t.
Corbis: Ocean, p. 14; Ingetje Tadros, p. 17b; KidStock/Blend Images, p. 22.
Getty Images: Logan Mock-Bunting, p. Cover.
Newspix: Patrina Malone, p. 5.
Shutterstock: pp. 1, 3, 6, 7, 8, 9(all), 10, 11br, 12, 13, 15, 16, 17t, 18(all), 20, 21, Back cover.

Every effort has been made to trace and acknowledge copyright. However, should any infringement have occurred, the publishers tender their apologies and invite copyright owners to contact them.

**Disclaimer**
Some of the images used in *Looking After Our Environment* might have associations with deceased Indigenous Australians. Please be aware that these images might cause sadness or distress in Aboriginal or Torres Strait Islander communities.

# Contents


Our world, our place 4

Damage done 6

Protecting the environment 10

A balancing act 14

Environmental innovation 18

Connections 22

Glossary 23

Index 24

# Our world, our place

An environment is an area of land, sea or air in which a person, animal or plant lives. It can occur naturally, like the ocean, or be man-made, like some parks.

Environments provide a home to all living things. They also provide food, water and shelter.

It is important to look after and protect the environment.

We need to be responsible and look after our environment so that future generations can live healthy lives within it too.

Looking after the environment sounds easy, but there are lots of things that must be considered.

**Did you know?**

If one environment is not looked after, the damage can be felt in other environments. The Great Barrier Reef suffers from pollution that comes from rivers flowing into the ocean.

**LET'S FIND OUT**

- **Why is the environment important?**
- **What impact is human activity having on the environment?**
- **Which environments should be protected?**
- **How do we balance human needs with environmental needs?**
- **Can we protect the environment by rethinking the way we do things?**

Sea Scouts help to clean up Doctor's Gully in Darwin, Northern Territory on Clean Up Australia Day.

# Damage done

Fossil fuels, burnt by heavy industry, produce greenhouse gases.

It only takes the actions of one person or **organisation** to cause great damage to an environment.

Here are five main ways in which different environments can be damaged:

### 1 Greenhouse gases

Heat comes to the Earth from the Sun. After warming the Earth, most of this heat leaves the Earth's atmosphere. However, some gases (called greenhouse gases) trap heat. These keep the Earth from becoming too cold. If there are too many of these gases in the atmosphere the Earth gets too warm. Burning **fossil fuels** produces greenhouse gases, which means the more fossil fuels that are burnt, the hotter the Earth will become. Some living things will not survive an increase in the Earth's temperature.

### 2 Oil spills

Oil is transported across oceans to countries around the world by huge oil tankers. Sometimes these tankers are involved in accidents. When this happens, millions of litres of thick black oil can spill into the ocean. Such an oil spill can be disastrous for the environment. It can injure and even kill plant and animal life in nearby water and along coastlines.

## 3 Deforestation

Deforestation is the cutting down of trees in forest areas. This process is also known as logging. The trees are cut down to provide timber for building houses and making furniture, paper and other items. Once these trees are removed many species of animals lose their homes and are at risk of becoming endangered. It also decreases the amount of oxygen that humans and other animals need to survive, because trees produce oxygen.

## 4 Chemicals in agriculture

Humans often use chemicals to protect their crops from insects, birds, fungi and other harmful pests that can destroy their produce. However, with rain and watering systems these chemicals often get washed into nearby waterways, damaging the environment and killing animal and plant life.

Chemicals, sprayed over crops by crop dusters, can end up in waterways.

## 5 Introducing invasive species

**Invasive** species are animals and plants that are taken from one environment and brought into another environment. Because they might not have a predator in their new environment, their numbers can get out of hand. Some invasive species end up as predators (hunters) of other native animals.

## Case study: Logging in Tasmania

For thousands of years, Eucalyptus trees have been part of the Tasmanian wilderness. They have nourished and sheltered many different species. However, since Europeans first settled Tasmania (then known as Van Diemen's Land) in the early 1800s, **logging** has been one of Tasmania's major industries.

Because of all the logging, 85 per cent of Tasmania's **old growth forests** have now disappeared. Old growth forests contain trees that can be several hundreds of years old. To save the remaining 15 per cent, an agreement was reached in 2011 between the **federal** government, the Tasmanian government, environmental groups and logging companies. The agreement meant that companies would stop logging in old growth forests. Instead, they would create more forests where they would plant new trees. These trees can then be cut down for timber after a few years and new ones planted in their place.

The aftermath of cutting down an old growth forest in Tasmania

### Case study: Gulf of Mexico oil spill 2010

In 2010, an oil rig exploded and sank in the Gulf of Mexico. Oil quickly spread across the ocean to the United States. This spill is the largest recorded in history. Oil polluted about 180 000 square kilometres of water and the coastline of the states of Louisiana, Mississippi, Alabama and Florida.

Oil spill workers collect tainted debris and dark oil patches along the beach as oil washes ashore on 10 June 2010 at Perdido Pass, Florida.

Thousands of marine creatures and birds were poisoned by the oil. When creatures were examined by scientists after the next breeding season, many were born dead or were smaller than normal. This event affected the entire food chain because there was less food for all the animals in that environment.

The spill was also a disaster for the people who depended on fishing for a living. Those working in tourism were also affected because fewer people came to stay along the damaged coastline.

# Protecting the environment

In some cases the environment can work to **regenerate** and create new life once it has been damaged. Natural disasters, such as fires, floods and earthquakes, have been damaging land for millions of years, before humans were even around. Today, even when a bushfire destroys an environment, new plants eventually grow, and animal species return to the area.

In many cases, however, environments need help and protection from humans if they are going to survive. This protection can be provided at local, national and international levels.

Planting new plants helps regenerate the environment.

## Local action

Local action involves individuals, communities and environmental groups putting plans into place to care for their environment.

Examples of local action include picking up litter, planting trees, removing weeds and monitoring the welfare of wildlife in the local area.

Students from Saint Ignatius College, Riverview, remove rubbish from the foreshore of Burns Bay, NSW, as part of Clean Up Australia Day.

### Clean up Australia

Clean Up Australia Day is an event that takes place on Australia Day (26 January) every year. It involves **volunteers** helping to clean up waterways and land in their local area.

In 1989, Ian Kiernan, a keen sailor, came up with the idea. After sailing around the world, he was shocked at the pollution he found wherever he went. When he returned to Sydney he and a friend, Kim McKay, organised the clean-up of Sydney Harbour. The following year all of Australia got on board to support Ian's great idea.

Clean Up Australia is an example of a program that started locally, became national and is now international. There is now a Clean Up the World Day that involves 35 million people in 120 countries.

## National action

National action involves the federal government passing laws to help care for the environment; for example, not allowing new buildings in national parks, or companies to drill for oil on the Great Barrier Reef. Without these laws many beautiful areas could be destroyed.

### National parks

The federal government has the power to declare environments as national parks. National parks are protected environments. They aim to **preserve** the plant and animal life within their boundaries. Farming is not allowed and people can only visit them for a short time. Plants and animals cannot be taken from a national park.

There are more than 500 national parks in Australia, covering about 4 per cent of the total land area.

The Breadknife rock formation in the Warrumbungles National Park, NSW

## International action

International action involves federal governments around the world working together to care for the environment. It can also include the work of world organisations, like the United Nations, to create World Heritage Sites.

### World Heritage Sites

These are buildings or environments that are unique. They are protected by special laws for the benefit of everyone worldwide. World Heritage Sites in Australia are:

1. Great Barrier Reef, QLD
2. Kakadu National Park, NT
3. Willandra Lakes Region, NSW
4. Lord Howe Island Group, NSW
5. Tasmanian Wilderness
6. Gondwana Rainforests of Australia, NSW
7. Uluru-Kata Tjuta National Park, NT
8. Wet Tropics of Queensland
9. Shark Bay, WA
10. Fraser Island, QLD
11. Heard and McDonald Islands, Antarctica
12. Macquarie Island, Antarctica
13. Greater Blue Mountains Area, NSW
14. Purnululu National Park, WA
15. Ningaloo Coast, WA

An aerial view of the Great Barrier Reef

# A balancing act

Would the environment be healthier if we didn't dig up the earth for mining? Would never cutting down another tree have a good impact on our lives?

While, ideally, we want a world that is as unspoiled as possible, human nature and human activity make it impossible to have a totally clean and untouched environment.

Imagine a world in which minerals remained in the ground because they were not allowed to be mined. Technologies such as computers, games consoles, furniture and transportation would not exist.

Now, imagine a world in which it was forbidden to cut down and use trees. Furniture, paper products and even pencils would not exist, making it very difficult to go about daily tasks.

It is important to keep a balance between preserving nature and allowing humans to make things important to their daily lives.

A careful balance is needed; one that understands that humans need **resources** from their environment, but that the environment needs constant care so that it can keep giving and surviving.

## The environment and the economy

Different environments play a big part in helping build the **economy**.

Tourism, mining, logging and the creation of products from natural materials help to create thousands of new jobs. These new jobs attract people to these areas. They provide income for the workers. They also encourage other people to visit and spend their money, often helping these towns to grow.

Uluru, one of Australia's top tourist destinations, exists within a fragile environment.

## Case study: The Gordon River

In the early 1980s, the Tasmanian government wanted to build a dam on the Gordon River to produce hydroelectricity (electricity created from falling water). People from all over Australia, and even overseas, protested against the dam, with over 2000 people joining a **blockade** to stop work from taking place. They were worried that the dam would damage the Gordon River. Its flow and surrounding land was unspoilt and home to hundreds of animal species.

However, a large number of people were in favour of the dam because the building work would create lots of jobs for its local people. It would also provide a cheaper source of electricity.

The federal government was very concerned about the environment and took the case to court. They won their hearing and the plans to build the dam were stopped.

Today, tourists visit the Franklin and Gordon rivers to admire the beautiful area. Many jobs have been created in the tourism industry.

The pristine and beautiful Gordon River in Tasmania was nearly dammed in the 1980s.

## Did you know?

The largest dam in the world is the Three Gorges Dam in China. While it produces an enormous amount of electricity, it has also stopped natural water flows, destroyed habitats along the routes of rivers, and resulted in soil erosion and landslides. More than one million people were forced to find somewhere else to live because the building of the dam destroyed their homes.

Building the Three Gorges Dam in China caused major environmental damage.

## Aboriginal people's relationship with the land

Aboriginal people have lived in Australia for more than 50 000 years. Over that time they have developed a very special connection and spiritual relationship with the land. The land and waterways of this country appear in Aboriginal Dreaming stories. The Dreaming refers to ancient times when the land and life were created. So harming the environment can do more than just physical damage; it can destroy areas that Aboriginal people consider to be **sacred**.

Growing concern over Broome Gas Reserve Area at James Price Point, WA, August 2011, led to protests.

# Environmental innovation

New technologies, research and ideas have changed the way we live, offering exciting new solutions for a **sustainable** world.

Solar powered radio

## Renewable energy

**Renewable** energy sources, such as solar (the Sun) and wind power, can reduce greenhouses gases and help keep the Earth cleaner.

## Sustainable forestry

Sustainable forestry involves planting trees for harvesting within a few years. This protects old forests containing trees that are hundreds of years old.

Sustainable forests contain trees that grow quickly and are easily harvested.

## Recycling

Today, many materials that could not be recycled in the past, and ended up as **landfill**, can now be recycled. Car tyres used to be dumped and burnt. The burning of tyres released dangerous gases into the environment. Today, car tyres are recycled and turned into artificial turf for sporting fields. Batteries, mobile phones and computers can also be recycled.

Some of the many items that can be recycled today

A biomass power plant in Poland

## Bio waste

Bio waste is the waste of dead plants and animals. Fossil fuels like oil and coal are bio wastes that take millions of years to form. Today, some people are using technology to turn plant and animal waste into energy.

Sawdust and shavings left over from logging can be mixed with chemicals and burnt in boilers to create steam to power electricity generators. These materials can also be turned into a liquid to use as fuel.

Waste from landfill and sewerage plants can also be broken down to produce methane gas. This gas can then be collected, stored and used to heat homes and create electricity.

## Case study: Wind farm

In Hepburn Springs, Victoria, the local community decided to create its own wind farm, to produce enough electricity for the area.

Over seven years meetings were held to teach the community about the plans and the reasons for change. The community chose a site on a nearby hill and got permission from the local council and the Victorian government. They found a company that could supply the turbine and, most importantly, they raised the millions of dollars needed to get the wind farm up and running.

In 2011 the wind farm was complete. This is a great example of how a community has taken action to create clean energy and reduce the amount of harmful greenhouses gases going into the atmosphere.

A wind farm in Victoria

# Connections

Environments are important for survival. They provide all living things with air, water, food and shelter. For humans, environments can provide a spiritual connection to people's history, culture and traditions. They can also be a great place to visit for a holiday. We have a responsibility to care for the environments on Earth for those living today and future generations. Here are some things we can do:

- Keep the Earth clean.
  For things to live and grow, the Earth needs to be kept clean. Make an effort to reduce pollution and deal with waste wisely.
- Look after our waterways.
  Clean water is essential for animal and plant life. Use water wisely and be responsible for what goes down the drain.
- Reduce air pollution.
  We all need clean fresh air to stay healthy. Make good choices about the energy sources and household products you use.

One way of keeping the environment clean is to pick up rubbish.

Every little action can make a difference to our world!

# Glossary

**blockade** blocking a passage or road to stop people or supplies from entering

**economy** the wealth of a country

**federal** national

**fossil fuels** the waste of plant and animal matter that has formed over millions of years, e.g. coal and oil

**invasive** tending to spread

**landfill** a space used for storing waste

**logging** cutting down forest trees for timber

**old growth forests** forests that contain many large, old, undisturbed trees, and often a variety of trees. They have never been logged

**organisation** a business, company or club formed for a particular purpose

**preserve** keep in good condition

**regenerate** to grow back

**renewable** able to be replaced by nature

**resources** things that grow that humans can use

**sacred** having a religious or spiritual purpose

**sustainable** able to be kept in the same state or at the same amount

**volunteers** people who do a task without being paid for it

# Index

**B**
bio waste 20
Burns Bay, NSW 11

**C**
chemicals 7
Clean Up Australia Day 5, 11

**D**
deforestation 7
Doctor's Gully, NT 5

**F**
fossil fuels 6, 20

**G**
Great Barrier Reef 4, 12, 13
greenhouse gases 6, 18, 21
Gordon River 16
Gulf of Mexico oil spill 9

**H**
Hepburn Springs, VIC 21
hydro-electricity 16

**I–K**
invasive species 7
James Price Point, WA 17
Kiernan, Ian 11

**L**
logging 7, 8, 15, 20

**M**
McKay, Kim 11
mining 14, 15

**N**
national parks 12

**O**
oil 6, 9, 12, 19, 20

**R**
recycling 19
renewable energy 18

**S**
sustainable forestry 18

**T**
Tasmanian Wilderness 8, 13, 16
Three Gorges Dam, China 17

**U**
Uluru-Kata Tjuta National Park, NT 13, 15
United Nations 13

**W**
Warrumbungles National Park 12
wind power 18, 21
World Heritage Sites 13